We find the amazing in the ordinary everyday, with lists, polls and quizzes. Helping us to appreciate, in fun and quirky ways, the world in which we live.

Creating interactive content, R Amazing! is a safe place to explore different topics and share your views.

It is ok to disagree with us regarding who or what we think is amazing! We share our thoughts on our website and in our books to enable debate and discussion.

We encourage the expression of opinions in an appropriate way with an understanding that it is ok for people to have differing views.

R Amazing! debates should be conducted politely and respectfully, ending with an agreement and common ground, even if that is to agree to disagree.

www.r-amazing.com

Odd Sports R Amazing!
Mark 'Markus' Baker & Adam Galvin

Published by R-and-Q.com.
Copyright © 2020 R-and-Q.com

This book is for informational purposes only.
We are NOT recommending trying these odd sports in any way.

Adam Galvin and Markus Baker
Creators of R Amazing!

ODD
SPORTS
AMAZING!

"*You have to be odd to be number one*"

Theodor Seuss Geisel

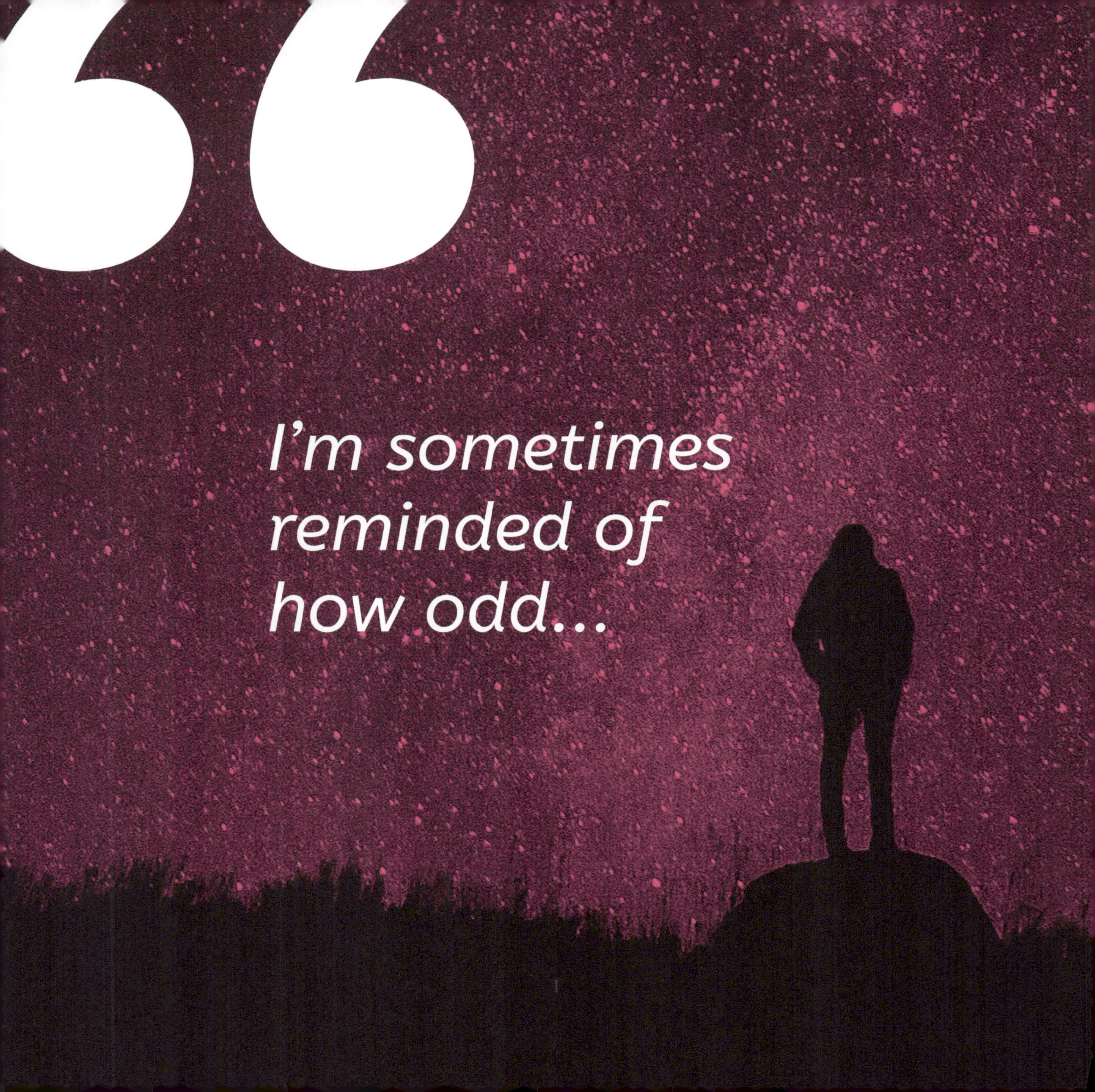

I'm sometimes
reminded of
how odd...

...I am, and how wonderful it is to be this way.

Maurice Sendak

LEARN MORE AT
www.r-amazing.com/chess-boxing/

Chess Boxing

As the title suggests, Chess Boxing is an eclectic mix of both chess and boxing! Opponents spar mentally as well as physically. Two competitors wear boxing attire and headphones whilst contemplating their chess moves in the middle of a boxing ring.

This game tests both competitor's brains and brawn – declaring a winner by checkmate in chess, technical knockout/knockout in boxing or disqualification by the referee for inactivity. A match lasts 11 alternating rounds – 6 rounds of chess and 5 of boxing.

Chess Boxing originates from Berlin in Germany, which started in 2003. The sport has gained momentum and is now more widespread around the world.

> *A computer once*
> *beat me at chess, but*
> *it was no match for*
> *me at kickboxing.*
> Emo Philips

LEARN MORE AT
www.r-amazing.com/extreme-ironing/

Extreme Ironing

The idea of Extreme Ironing, also known as EI, was created out of boredom in 1997. As a small act of rebellion, Phil Shaw from Leicester in the UK, took his ironing board into the garden.

Since EI's inception, it has grown beyond Phil's imagination: Ironing on cliff faces upside down, pressing in the forest, even in the sea, whilst windsurfing, paragliding, riding a bike, water rapid boating, skiing and even whilst abseiling!

In 2002, the 1st Extreme Ironing Championships took place in Valley, Bavaria, a small village near Munich in Germany. This competition comprised of 12 teams from 10 different nations. Competitors were tested on their ability to endure 5 ironing tests on a variety of fabrics in different arduous environments ranging from rocky, forest, urban and water.

The documentary, Extreme Ironing: Pressing for Victory, gained international sporting attention. In 2016, Extreme Ironing was recognised as an official sport by De Montfort University in Leicester.

> *The latest danger sport that combines the thrills of an extreme outdoor activity with the satisfaction of a well-pressed shirt.*
>
> Extreme Ironing Bureau

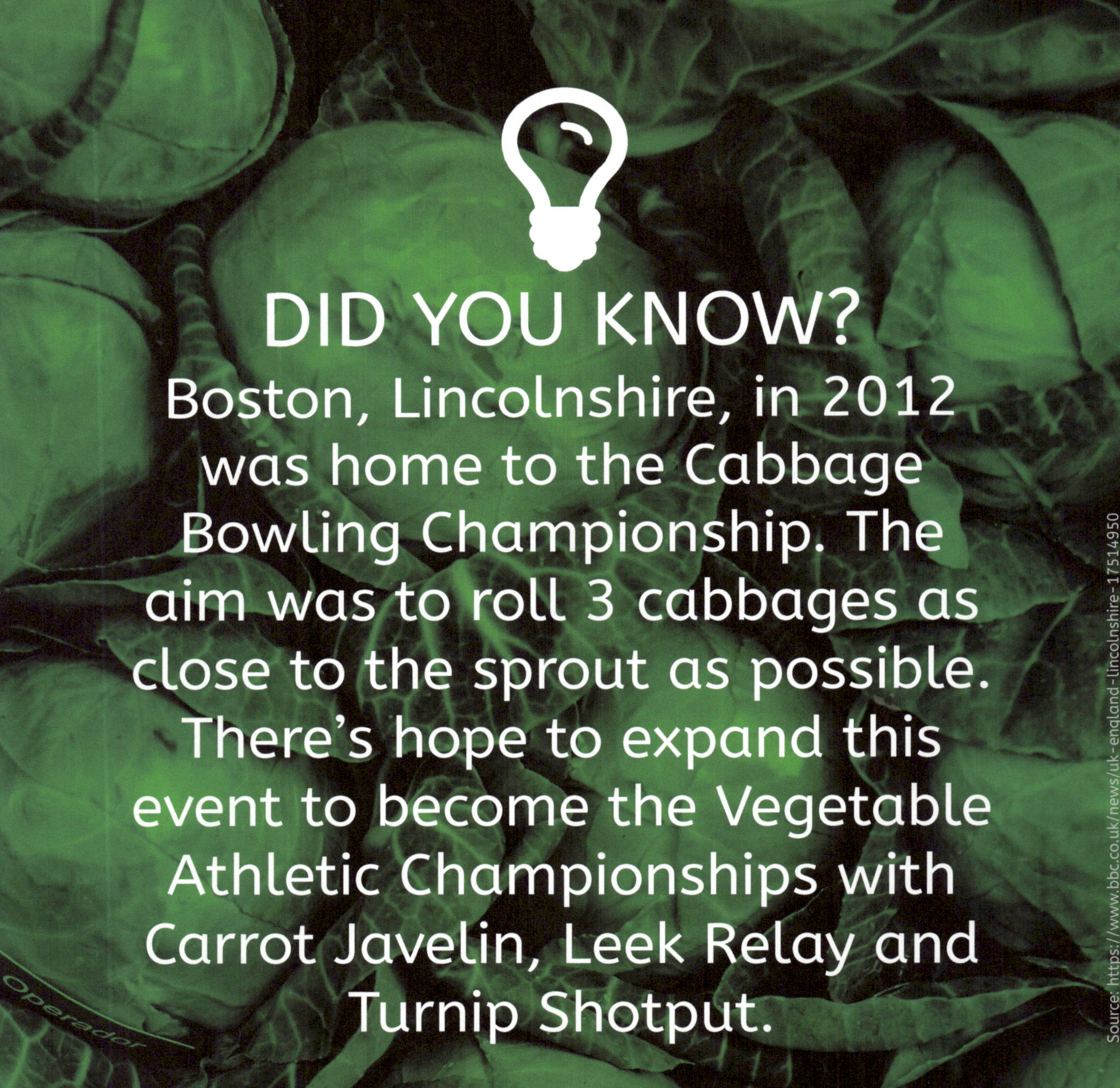
DID YOU KNOW?
Boston, Lincolnshire, in 2012 was home to the Cabbage Bowling Championship. The aim was to roll 3 cabbages as close to the sprout as possible. There's hope to expand this event to become the Vegetable Athletic Championships with Carrot Javelin, Leek Relay and Turnip Shotput.
Source: https://www.bbc.co.uk/news/uk-england-lincolnshire-17514950

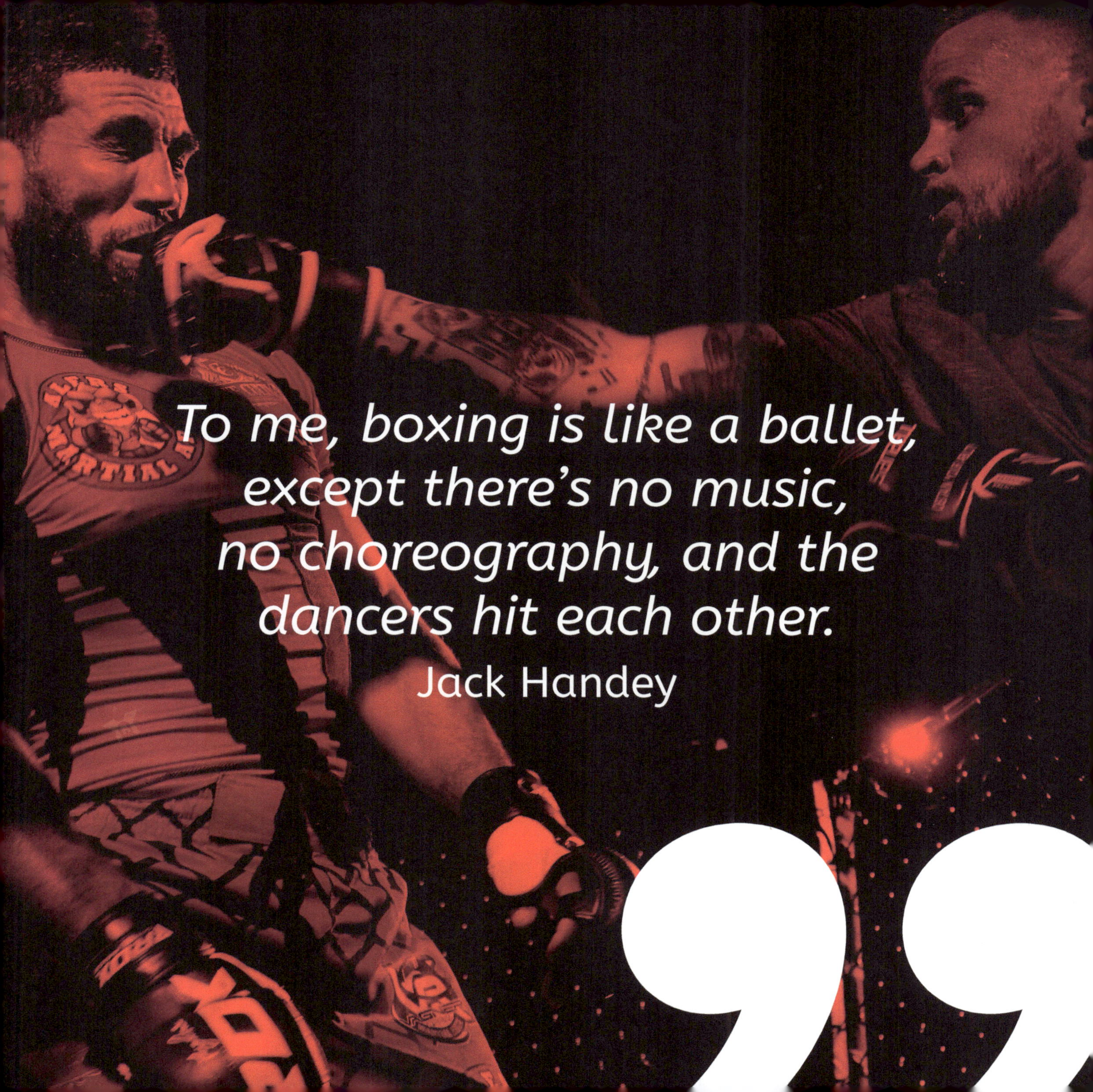
To me, boxing is like a ballet, except there's no music, no choreography, and the dancers hit each other.
Jack Handey

LEARN MORE AT
www.r-amazing.com/cheese-rolling/

Cheese Rolling

Cheese rolling is believed to have been around for hundreds of years, even dating back to pre-Roman times. It is thought to be one of the oldest customs to have survived through the history of Great Britain.

Each year the crowds turn out in large numbers at Cooper's Hill in Gloucestershire, showing that it is still as popular today as it ever has been. Even though it looks fun, participants risk life and limb chasing the 7lb double Gloucester cheese. Many say that participating is the absolute adrenaline thrill of taking on such a steep and dangerous decline.

Before the competitors race down the hill, the cheese gets a 1 second head start. The winner is the person holding the cheese whilst crossing the finishing line. Their prize is to keep the cheese along with the accolade of being crowned the Cheese Rolling Champion for that year.

Often there are injuries such as sprains and a number of broken bones. However, all those who take part in the exciting and extreme race believe it is a risk worth taking.

LEARN MORE AT
www.r-amazing.com/worm-charming/

Worm Charming

In 1980, The World Worm Charming Championships began in the village of Willaston in Northern England. Due to boredom, a group of people decided to compete against each other to see who could conjure the most worms out of the ground. Since then it has grown in popularity with competitors coming from as far as Europe to take part or spectate.

Each worm charming team are given a 3×3 metre plot. They are instructed that no digging is allowed and all worms must be returned to the ground totally unharmed after the competition has finished.

Competitors of worm charming attempt to entice as many worms as they can to the surface within a 30 minute time limit. There are many methods used to coerce worms to the surface which include: creating vibrations, imitating the sound of rain, playing the sound of rainfall and even using non-toxic liquid mixtures. Once out of the ground the worms are placed into a plastic container ready for counting.

Worm charming's official judge, known as the 'Worm Master' ensures the 18 rules are followed. Each team is made up of three people: a Charmerer, a Pickerer and a Counterer.

In just half-an-hour, 10-year-old Sophie Smith charmed a record breaking 567 worms from the ground during the 2009 World Worm Charming Championships.

In order to start winning,
we have to stop losing.
Emmanuel Arceneaux

DID YOU KNOW?

Tualatin, Oregon holds a very unique rowing Regatta each October. The contestants each hollow out a large Pumpkin, dress in fun Halloween costumes to race across Tualatin Lake.

LEARN MORE AT
www.r-amazing.com/egg-throwing/

Egg Throwing

The World Egg Throwing Championships takes place in Swaton, England at the end of June each year. It is believed to have originated in 1322 when Swaton's new abbot encouraged church attendance by giving out eggs. When the nearby river flooded, preventing people from attending church, the monks threw the eggs across the river. Over the next 700 years the townspeople took part in the fun.

It costs 4 British Pounds to enter and is regulated by the World Egg Throwing Federation who ensure all eggs are organic, free-range and sustainably sourced.

The World Egg Throwing Championships has 5 options to compete in:

1. Egg throwing and catching – over greater distances, a team of two throw and catch an egg without dropping it

2. Static egg relay – where throwers pass a dozen eggs as quickly as they can down the line

3. Egg trebuchet – teams build a catapulting machine and launch eggs at opposing team members

4. Egg accuracy – Thrown at a person: Head shot = Nil pts, Arms/legs=1 pt, Body = 2 pts & Groin = 3 pts

5. Russian egg roulette – two competitors choose from 6 eggs and take it in turns to smash it against their forehead. Five are hard-boiled; one is raw.

LEARN MORE AT
www.r-amazing.com/gurning/

Gurning Contests

Since 1267, Egremont Crab Fair has been held in mid-september to give away away crab apples. One of its main attractions is The World Gurning Championships. Gurning is a British word that means to pull an odd facial expression.

Participants place their head through a horse collar and pull the strangest face they can.

The champions are the man and woman who are judged to have 'Gurned' the best. Tommy Mattinson and Anne Woods are both gurning legends who between them have won over 40 World Championships.

As you are reading this now, why not 'gurn' the funniest face you can and see if anybody notices?

Crab apples are very bitter and when you eat something bitter your face contorts. That's how gurning started and gurning contests have been around ever since.

Karen Clement
Event Organiser

DID YOU KNOW?

Since 1996, The redneck games have been taking place in East Dublin, Georgia.
Events include Bobbing for pig's feet, Seed spitting, Toilet seat throwing, Mud pit belly flop, Big-hair contest, Armpit serenade, Dumpster diving and Hubcap hurling to name but a few.

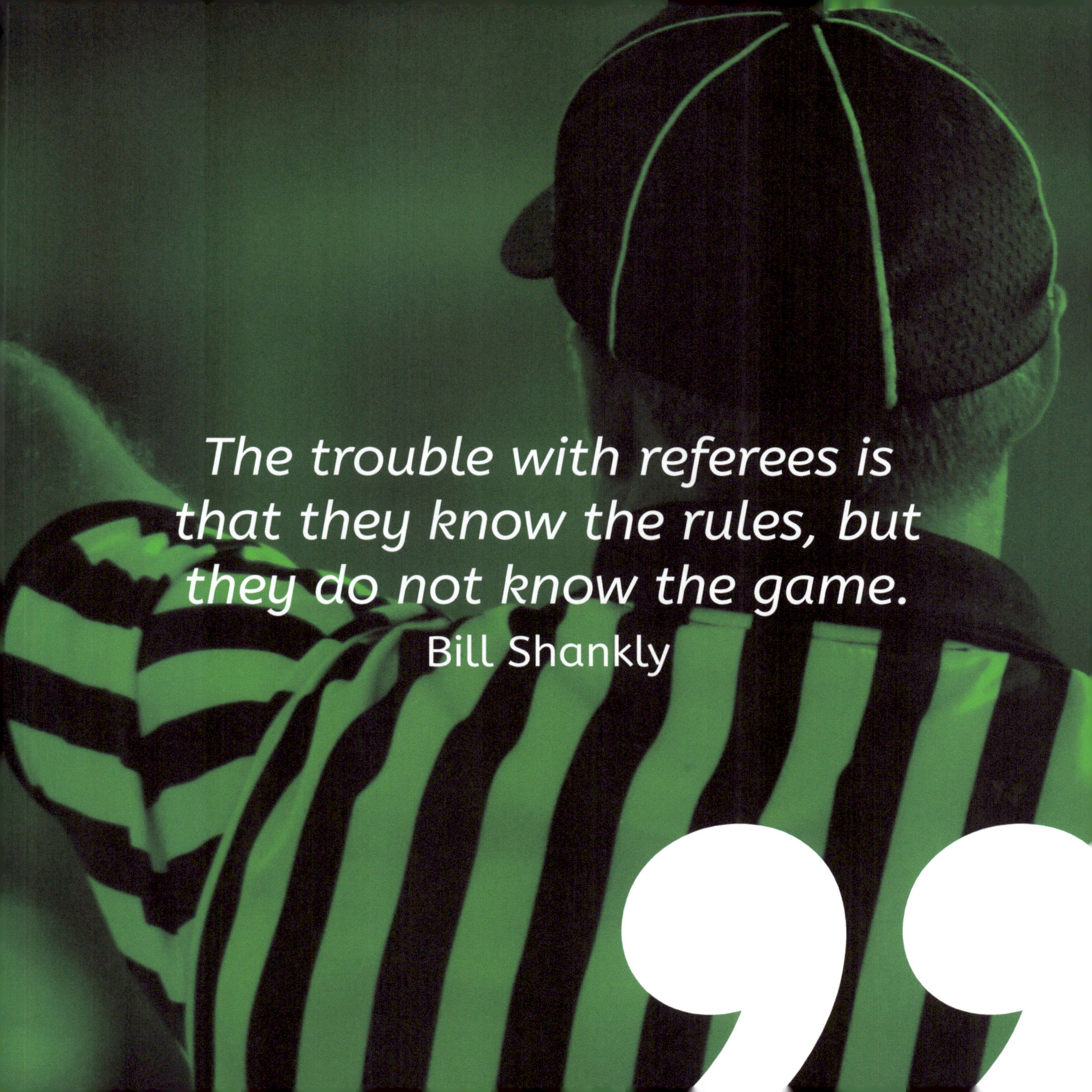

The trouble with referees is that they know the rules, but they do not know the game.
Bill Shankly

LEARN MORE AT
www.r-amazing.com/lawnmower-race/

Lawnmower Racing

Back in 1973, the sport of Lawnmower Racing was created by Jim Gavin along with the help of a few pints in a West Sussex country pub. He wanted to start a motorsport that didn't involve lots of money or sponsors and that was readily accessible to all.

After watching a local groundsman mowing the green, it dawned on him that nearly everyone has a lawnmower in their shed. It was arranged that a race would be held in Murphy's Field and to everyone's astonishment around 80 lawnmowers turned up to compete.

Lawnmower racing has attracted a range of celebrities and past motor racing legends, with the likes of Sir Stirling Moss who has won both the British Lawn Mower Racing Association's British Grand Prix and 12-Hour Races.

Heralded as the cheapest motosport in the UK, there are still no sponsorships, no commercialism, no cash purses and competitors are not allowed to modify their engines. The British Lawnmower Racing Association believes this keeps costs down as a non-profit organisation.

On Your Mark,
Get Set,
MOW!
Mike Ratel

LEARN MORE AT
www.r-amazing.com/hobby-horsing/

Hobby Horsing

Similar to show jumping and dressage except the humans participants are not riding real life horses. Instead they use an imaginary one called a hobby horse, which is a wooden pole with a stuffed fabric horse head on the end.

Although hobby horses have been around since the 16th Century, their popularity had declined massively. This changed when young girls in Finland developed Hobby Horsing. A sport that, like ballet, requires a mix of speed, strength and athleticism.

From its humble beginnings in Finland, this sport's popularity has grown so much that it now requires judges and coaches, and has spread its reach into Sweden, Russia and the Netherlands.

Most of the participants are young girls who feel this sport is a way for them to express themselves. In 2017, Selma Vilhunen, directed a humorous and touching documentary that shared how teenagers found their voice through participating in Hobby Horsing.

It has helped me a great deal that I can occasionally just go galloping into the woods with my friends. It somehow balances my mind.

Alisa Aarniomaki

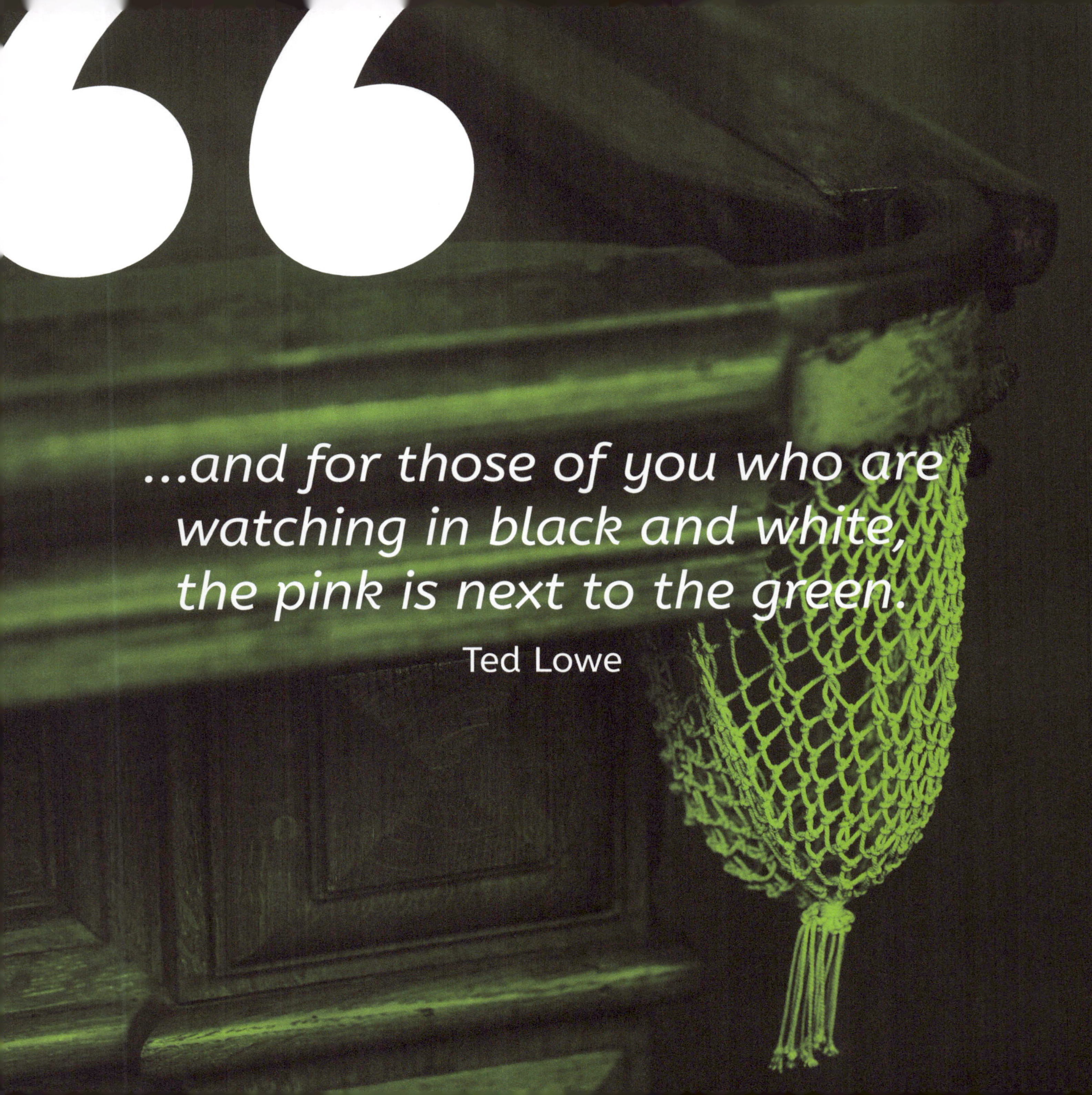

...and for those of you who are watching in black and white, the pink is next to the green.
Ted Lowe

DID YOU KNOW?

Fierljeppen which roughly translates from its Dutch origins as "far leaping". Similar to pole vault though instead of seeing how high, the aim is to see how far you can sling yourself.

LEARN MORE AT
www.r-amazing.com/toe-wrestling/

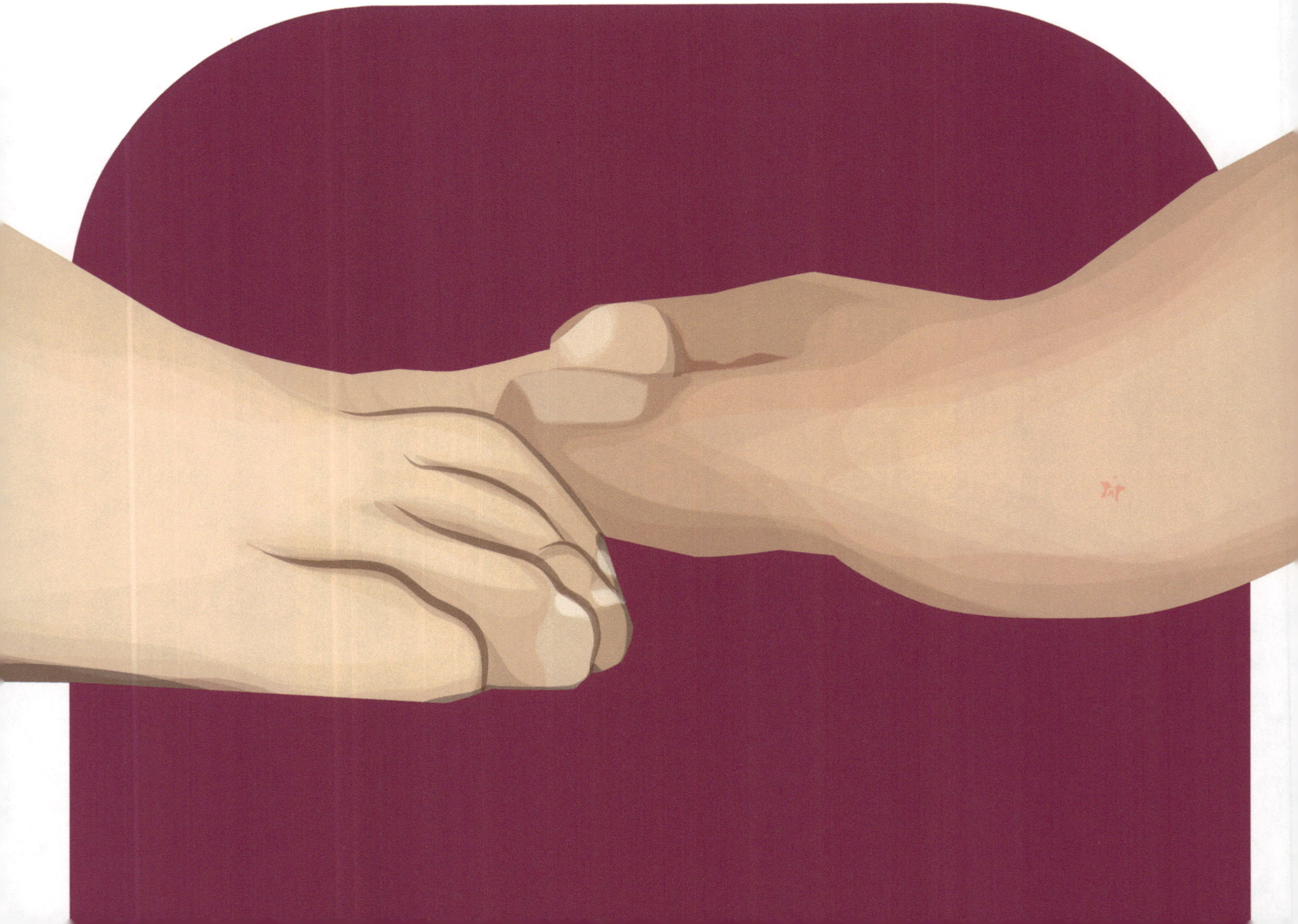

Toe Wrestling

Back in 1974 the UK did not have many World Champions. So four drinkers at the Ye Olde Royal Oak Inn in Wetton, Staffordshire decided to invent a sport that no other country knew about. Thus ensuring Great Britain would have 3 new world champions Mens, Womens and Childrens. This worked well until 1976 when a Canadian won the Men's championship.

Before settling on Toe Wrestling, the quartet had considered ear wrestling and push of war which would use a scaffolding pole instead of a rope.

The rules of toe wrestling are that competitors must have their bottom and both hands on the floor at all times. The leg that is not being used to wrestle needs to be held up off the ground. Players must be bare footed and their toes must be flat against their opponents toes. There are three rounds and the winner is the first person to pin their opponent's foot for three seconds twice.

This sport can be challenging. Once a competitor named Alan "Nasty" Nash broke four toes in his semi final match, but still somehow managed to go on to win the championship.

Looking to expand to the masses, organizers in 1997 applied for toe wrestling's inclusion into the Olympic Games, unfortunately they were not successful.

LEARN MORE AT
www.r-amazing.com/bo-taoshi/
30° angle
30° angle

Bo-Taoshi

Literally translated as pole bringing-down, Bo -Taoshi is a traditional Japanese game whose history is relatively unknown and somewhat mysterious. It is thought that it was first played by the Japanese military around 1945. Bo-Taoshi has the lure of combat sports with its chaotic, aggressive and fast pace that keep the fans coming back for more.

Bo-Taoshi involves two teams of 150 players, each team is then split into half to create attacker and defender groups. The defensive group tactically position themselves around their pole. When ready, they signal by raising their hands.

As soon as a gunshot is heard, the attacking groups from the opposing teams rush to try and topple their opponents pole before their own pole is toppled.

The winner is the team that is the first to lower their opponent's pole to the angle of 30 degrees or below.

It is impressive that there are no serious accidents.
Satoshi Matsumoto

DID YOU KNOW?

After remembering how much he enjoyed mock sword fights used to be, Robert Easley from Seattle, Washington started the Cardboard Tube Fighting League. With the added bonus of nobody getting cut, hurt or killed like in real sword fights, this league has one purpose and that is to have as much fun as possible.

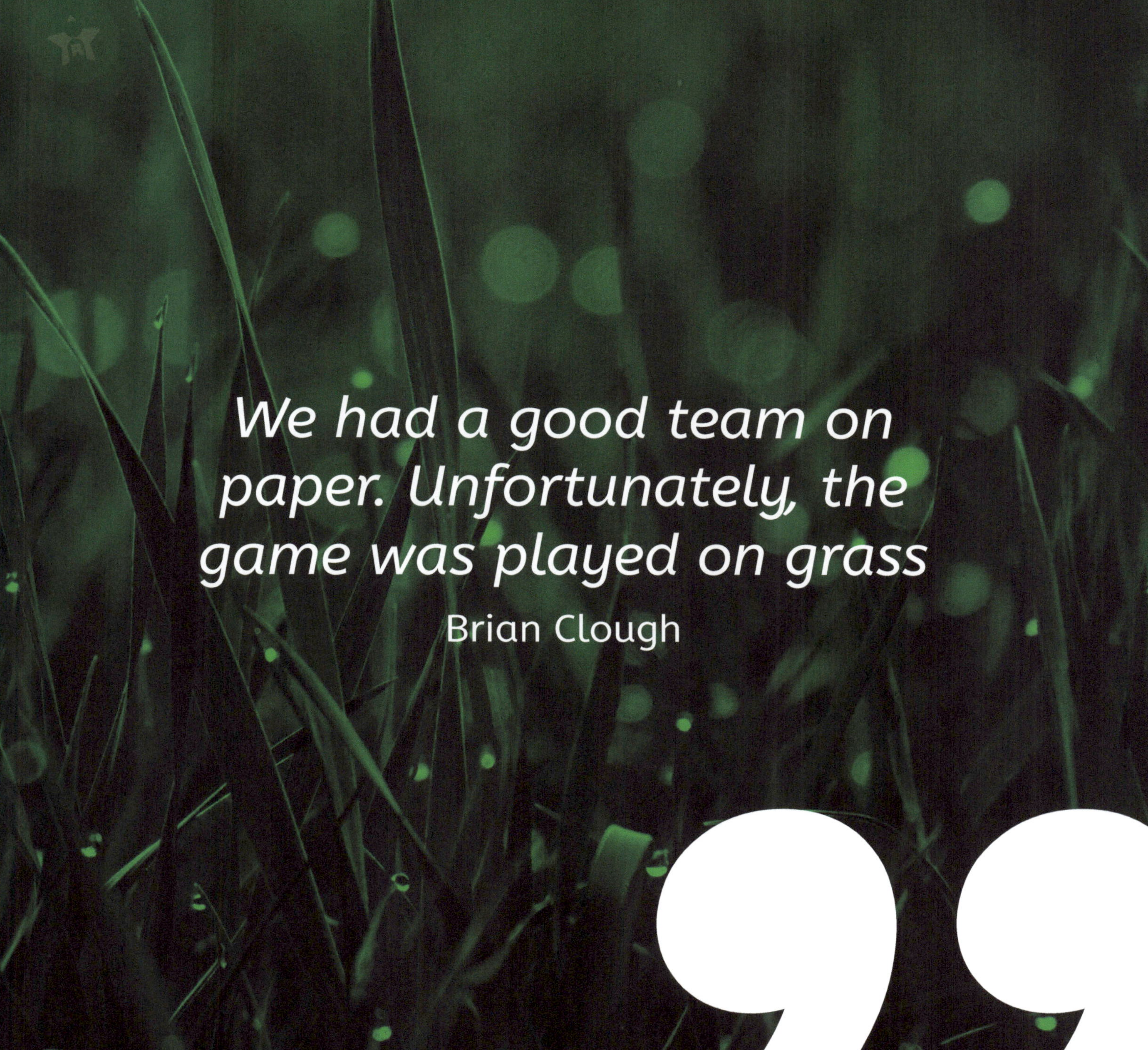
We had a good team on paper. Unfortunately, the game was played on grass
Brian Clough

LEARN MORE AT
www.r-amazing.com/ferret-legging/

Ferret Legging

Two ferrets with razor sharp claws and teeth, check! A human wearing a pair of trousers (pants) that are tied at the bottom, check! A judge with a stopwatch, check!

You may have guessed what happens next in the sport of Ferret Legging. Yes, the ferrets are put into the person's trousers. The judge then times to see how long the participant can last before they need to take the ferrets out of their trousers to relieve themselves from the pain of their scratched and bitten legs (and other bits!).

From 1972, when the record was 40 seconds, it gradually increased upto 1981 when retired coal miner, Reg Mellor broke it with an astounding 5 hours and 26 minutes. A record he held until 2010, when Frank Bartlett, a retired headmaster, and Christine Farnsworth raised £1,000 for the Whittington Community First Responders by completing an amazing five hours and thirty minutes.

A centuries old sport that had a brief revival in the 1970's, Ferret-legging has now become increasingly irrelevant due the lack of participants and the animal welfare concerns for the ferret's wellbeing.

> *No filing of the teeth; no clipping.*
> *No dope for you or the ferrets.*
> *You must be sober, & the ferrets*
> *must be hungry.*
>
> Reg Mellor

I've never lost a game,
I just ran out of time.
Michael Jordan

DID YOU KNOW?

To win at Shin Kicking your opponent must give up by saying either 'Enough' or "Sufficient". A match is the best of 10, meaning the first to reach 6 wins takes the match. Participants have to hold each other's collar and can only kick with the inside of their foot.

My picture of the most amazing odd sport in the world!

The most amazing odd sport in the world is

. . . .

My favourite part of this amazing odd sport is...

. . . .

. . . .

. . . .

. . . .

. . . .

. . . .

This odd sport is amazing because...

. . . .

. . . .

. . . .

. . . .

MORE BOOKS BY R&Q

check out the books and merchandise at

w w w . R - a n d - Q . c o m